# Gray Bats and YOU

By Tasha V. Gabel

ISBN-13: 978-1514600375
ISBN-10: 1514600374

# Dedication

This book is dedicated to my daughter and all children of future generations. Nature has been here long before us, it surrounds us now, and it will be here long after us. My hope is that this book helps children see that nature is not something we should conquer, but something we should enjoy.

Hello! I am Gracie the Gray Bat. I am here to tell you some facts about me.

Let me take you on an adventure to the world I know!

First of all, there are many types of bats all over the world. Some are big with a wingspan the size of a grown man!

Others are small like the Bumble Bee Bat, which is the size of a bumble bee!

Some things all bats have in common are that we are the only flying mammal and we all love to sleep upside down.

We sleep upside down so that we can fly away easily when we wake up.

Now let's fly to where I live! In the United States, Gray Bats live in states like Alabama, Kentucky, Arkansas, Missouri, and Tennessee.

Are any of these states one *you* live in? If so, I may be your neighbor!

Caves may be spooky to some people and animals, but we Gray Bats love caves!

Caves give us a place to hibernate. When we hibernate we shut down our bodies all winter long.

Cave ceilings allow us to hang by our feet. Caves also give us shelter and keep us safe from predators that might eat us for a snack!

Speaking of snacks, let's get one of my favorite meals...mosquitoes! I come out at night and eat mosquitoes and other flying insects.

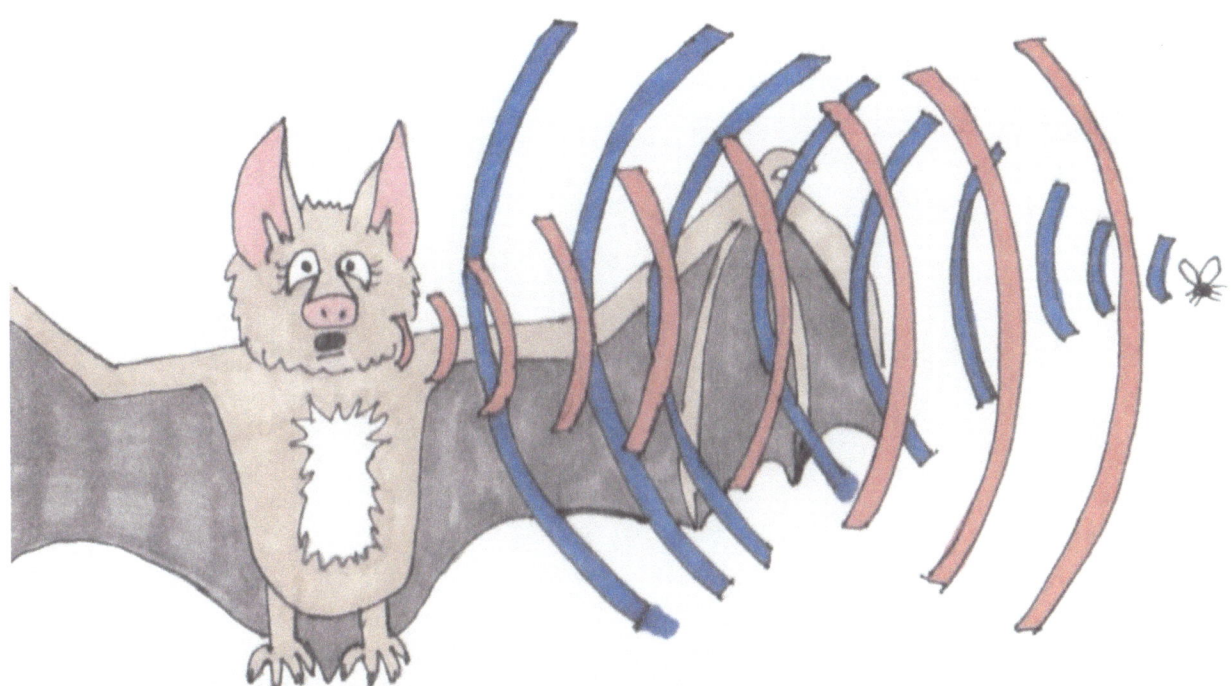

I use echolocation to catch my prey in the dark of the night. Instead of using my eyes to hunt, I make click and squeak noises with my mouth. The noises bounce off my prey and back to my ears and that is how I know exactly where my prey is even in the dark.

There are not many people that I know who like mosquitoes, and my Gray Bat friends and I keep the mosquito numbers down for you! You are welcome!

Now, if you remember, I said that some creatures like bats for a snack like I like insects for a snack. This helps all of my wildlife friends stay in balance with each other.

We bats keep the insect numbers manageable and our predators keep our numbers manageable. With a system like that there is no way one animal will take over!

Two of our many predators are owls and snakes. We bats may have some cool tricks, but our predators have some super powers of their own!

Snakes hang out in holes in cave walls and wait for one of us to fly by. If we fly too closely to the snake's hiding spot, we could get snatched up!

Gray Bats cannot see very well and use echolocation to fly in the night, but owls have very good eye sight at night.

As sneaky as we may be, we have to be very careful when flying around owls at night. They are very alert and always hungry!

I know some people are scared of bats so I want to tell you a secret about us...we are actually pretty cute and no threat to people at all!

Bats rarely come near humans, but if one does happen to fly by your head don't worry! Bats know exactly where you are because of echolocation. We will avoid you as best as we can because we really don't want to run into you either.

We bats may be hard to spot in the wild, so you should be excited if you do see one of us!

Here is something interesting you may not have known about Gray Bats: Gray Bat mothers only have one pup a year. The mother raises her baby for about one month, which is about the time the baby starts to fly on its own.

Gray Bat mothers also carry their pups on their backs until the pups are ready to fly by themselves. Imagine your mom having to carry *you* on *her* back all the time!

Bats all over the world help our planet in many ways! Like I said before, we help to control those pesky insects that bite, sting, and buzz.

We play an important role in the food chain, and we keep the ecosystem in balance when we are both inside and outside of caves.

Now that you know a little about Gray Bats, can you imagine if we were not around? I imagine that most of the insects we eat would still be around to bug you!

Insects do more than just bug you. If it were not for bats like me the insects could take over and spread diseases! These diseases could make you humans really sick.

Speaking of feeling sick, some Gray Bats and other types of bats have not been feeling too well lately. I am sad to say that we have some bad news for Gray Bats.

A lot of us are sick from White Nose Syndrome (WNS).

White Nose Syndrome is a fungus that grows on us in caves that looks like powder has been sprinkled on our noses and wings. This fungus makes us pretty thirsty and weak. The fungus is very itchy too, like wearing a wool sweater *all the time*!

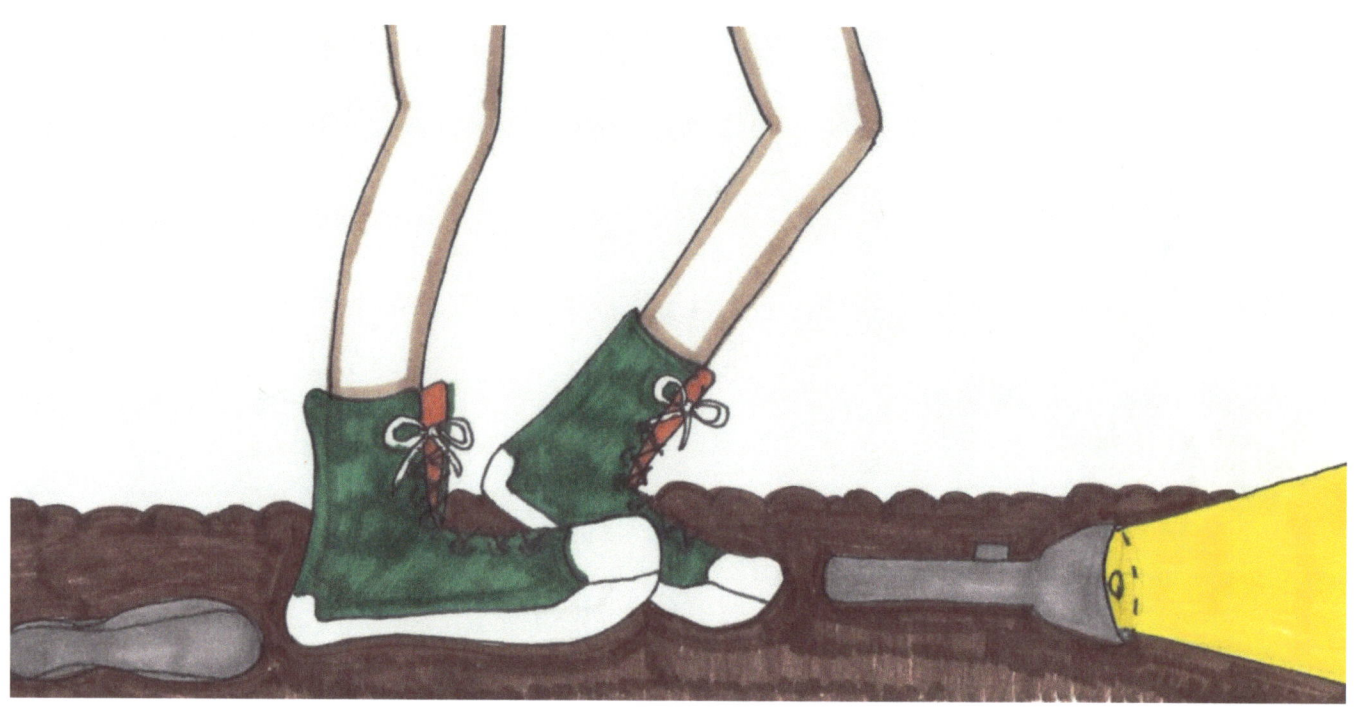

Humans can bring this fungus into caves on their clothing, shoes, or anything they bring with them if they have been in another cave with White Nose Syndrome.

It is very important to properly disinfect your clothes and equipment if you may have been in a cave with WNS before you enter another cave. This helps to stop the spread of this horrible fungus!

There is some hope for us Gray Bats because people like you are always learning and trying to help Gray Bats out!

How you can help is to stay out of caves unless you are led by a trained park guide. You can also spread the word and tell all of your friends what you learned here today.

Well, my human friend, it is time for me to fly away. I had a great time teaching you about Gray Bats!

The more you learn about nature, the more you can enjoy it! Never stop learning about wildlife and YOU!

## About the Author

My name is Tasha Gabel and I studied Wildlife Conservation and Management at Missouri State University. I have worked as a naturalist at Meramec State Park where I led cave tours, nature hikes, and river wades. I have also worked for the fishery and forestry departments for the Missouri Department of Conservation.

I enjoy nature and I strive to help people of all ages learn about and respect the natural world around them. Much of my free time is dedicated to birding, kayaking, and camping. I also enjoy the company of my husband and two dogs.

In October my husband and I will have a new addition in our family. My *Wildlife and You* book series is dedicated to our future daughter, as well as to children all over. I believe it is important to teach children to enjoy the outdoors because this will better ensure that there will still be wildlife for generations to come.

Thank you for reading my book, and thank you even more for being a fan of nature!